Nine Men Chase a Hen

**Written by
Barbara Gregorich**

**Illustrated by
John Sandford**

One hen wants a hat.

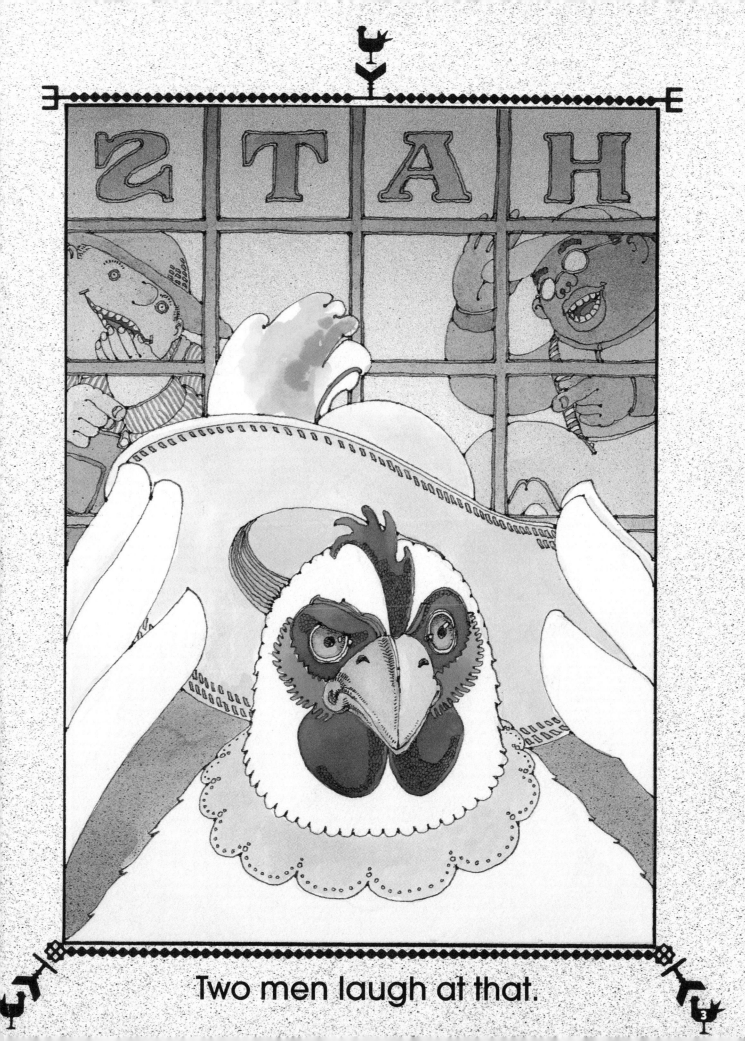

Two men laugh at that.

Three men have a pet.

Four hens get very wet.

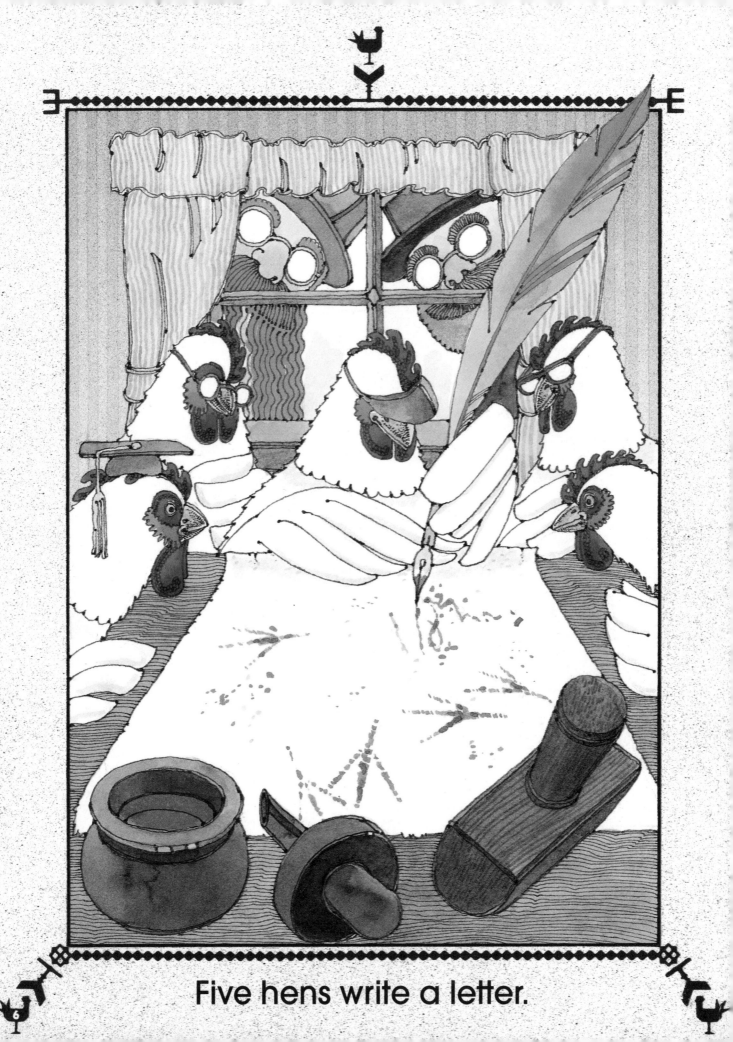

Five hens write a letter.

Six men say theirs is better.

Seven men sleep at night.

Eight hens make it light.

Nine men chase a hen.

Ten hens chase the men.

All the men run away.

All the hens begin to play.

Now this funny story ends.

All the men and hens are friends.

The End

Jog, Frog, Jog

Written by
Barbara Gregorich

Illustrated by
Rex Schneider

This is a frog.

The frog likes to jog.

He jogs in the day.

He jogs in the night.

Oh, Oh! This is a dog.

The dog does not like frogs.

The dog sees the frog!

Jog, frog, jog!

Jog in the water.

Jog in the fog.

Go, frog, go!

Jog into the log!

The log stops the dog.

Jog, frog. Jog around that dog.

Let's Do More with *Nine Men Chase a Hen*

Men and Hens

Take turns with your child to continue the story, following the rhyming pattern to sixteen men—or even twenty. Here are some possibilities to get you started:

> Eleven men start to sneeze.
> Twelve hens float in the breeze.
> Thirteen men dig a hole.
> Fourteen hens see a mole.
> Fifteen men scratch their head.
> Sixteen hens eat cheese and bread.

Encourage your child to illustrate the new rhymes.

Story Math

Nine Men Chase a Hen provides an appealing and convenient way to practice counting, as well as a good source of story problems. Have your child choose a page from the story. Ask him or her to count the men, the hens, and any other animals in the illustration. (Watch out: a rabbit is hiding in several of the pictures.) How many in all? Encourage your child to write addition problems, either with pictures or numbers, that show the men, the animals, and the total.

Rhyming Word Wall Chart

Make a word chart for rhymes in the story that generate the greatest number of additional rhyming words and have the most common spelling patterns (*hat/that, pet/wet, hen/men*). Write the pairs of words at the top of columns on a large sheet of paper. Hang the chart on a wall. Then ask your child to add rhyming words as he or she hears or reads them to the appropriate columns on the chart.

Let's Do More with *Jog, Frog, Jog*

Design a T-Shirt

Can your child read the frog's T-shirt? What other symbols can stand for words (1 = won, 4 = for or fore, 8 = ate, ⊘ = no, ● = stop, and so on)?

Have your child think of a slogan for a T-shirt that includes symbols. Then encourage him or her to draw a T-shirt with this slogan. If you have an old T-shirt on hand, your child can write the slogan on the shirt with fabric paint or colored markers.

Other Places, Other Weather

Ask your child to think of other places the frog might jog and other kinds of weather in which he might find himself. Have your child illustrate the frog and the appropriate background. Ask your child to write or dictate a sentence that describes where the frog is or what the weather is like. For example, your child might draw the frog jogging through a forest and write, "The frog jogs in the woods." Or the child might draw a frog jogging through a snowstorm and write, "The frog jogs in the snow."

What Is a Frog?

Help your child list some of the things he or she knows about frogs. If the child doesn't mention the following facts, share some of this information:

Frogs have moist green or brown skin. They are amphibians, cold-blooded animals with backbones that live in water and breathe through gills when they are young. As adults, they develop lungs and live on land.

Frogs grow from eggs that float in the water to tadpoles with long tails that breathe through gills. As they get older, tadpoles grow legs. Eventually tadpoles lose their tails, emerge from the water, and become adult frogs.

Many children are interested in the life stages of frogs. Help your child find out more about frogs from direct observation or from books. Encourage your child to draw pictures of frogs and write about them.

Come to Dilly's birthday party!

_____

- -

To: _____

your first name.

Where: 12 Bailey Road

When: 1:00 Saturday, May 3

What time is Dilly's party?

the hands on the clock.

◯ the date of Dilly's party.

May 13   May 23   May 3

Dilly's invitation.

34

Dilly is dressed for his party.

Dilly's 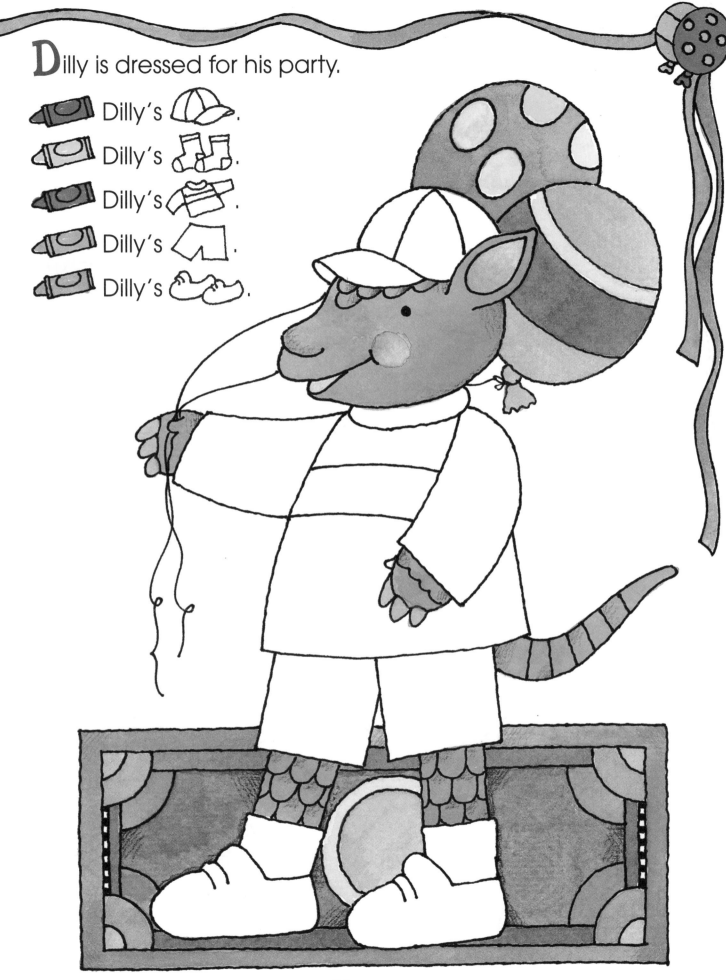.

Dilly's .

Dilly's .

Dilly's .

Dilly's .

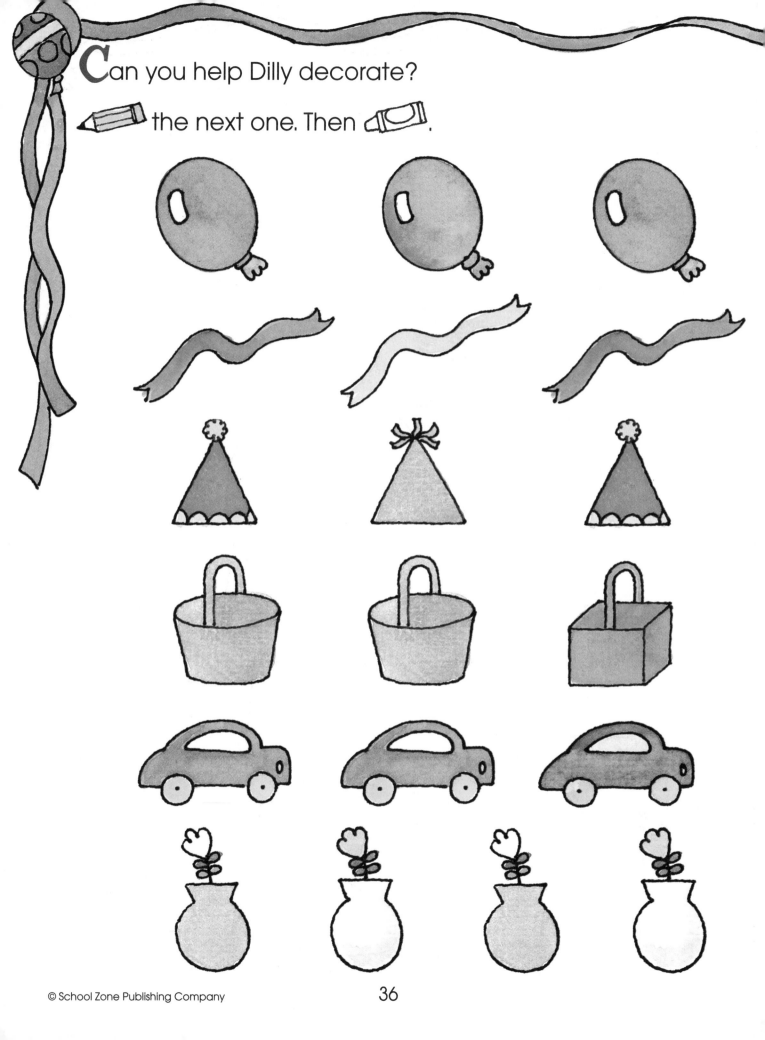

Can you help Dilly decorate?

the next one. Then.

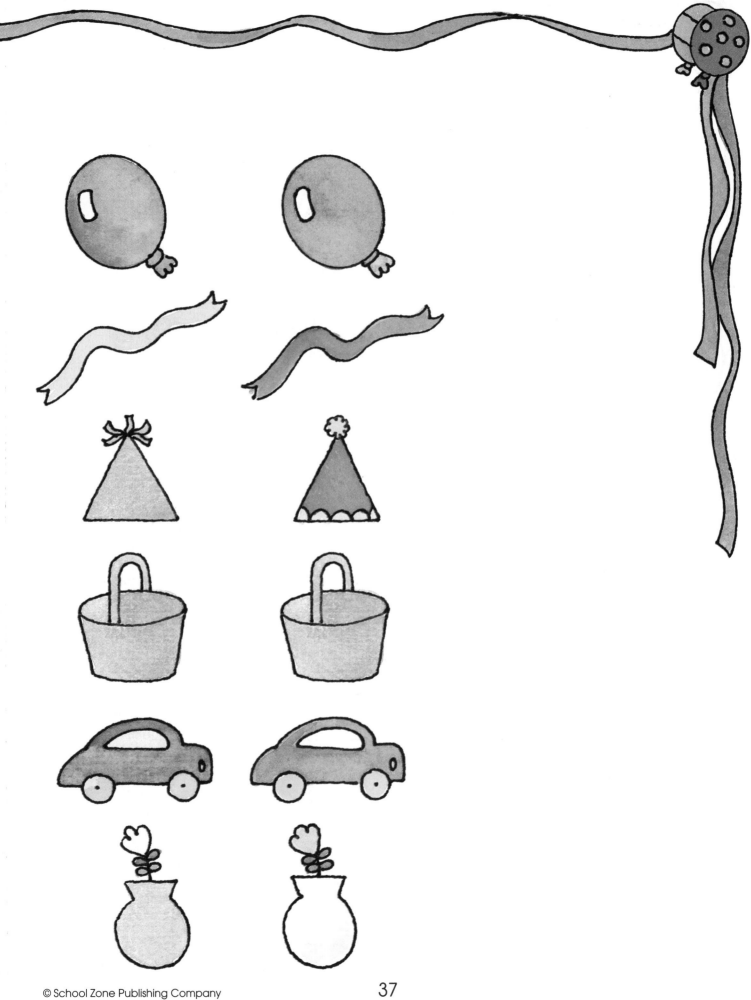

Take Ruben, Lola, and Shari to Dilly's house.

a line from Ruben's house.

a line from Lola's house.

a line from Shari's house

shari

Lola

39

The guests are here!

the ☐ s.

the △ s.

the ◯ s.

Then the rest of the picture.

Want to play some games?
What happens first, next, last?
✏️ 1, 2, 3.

Who is breaking the piñata?

How many s? How many s?

How many s? Fill in the ☐s.

	1	2	3	4	5	6	7	8

Play drop the 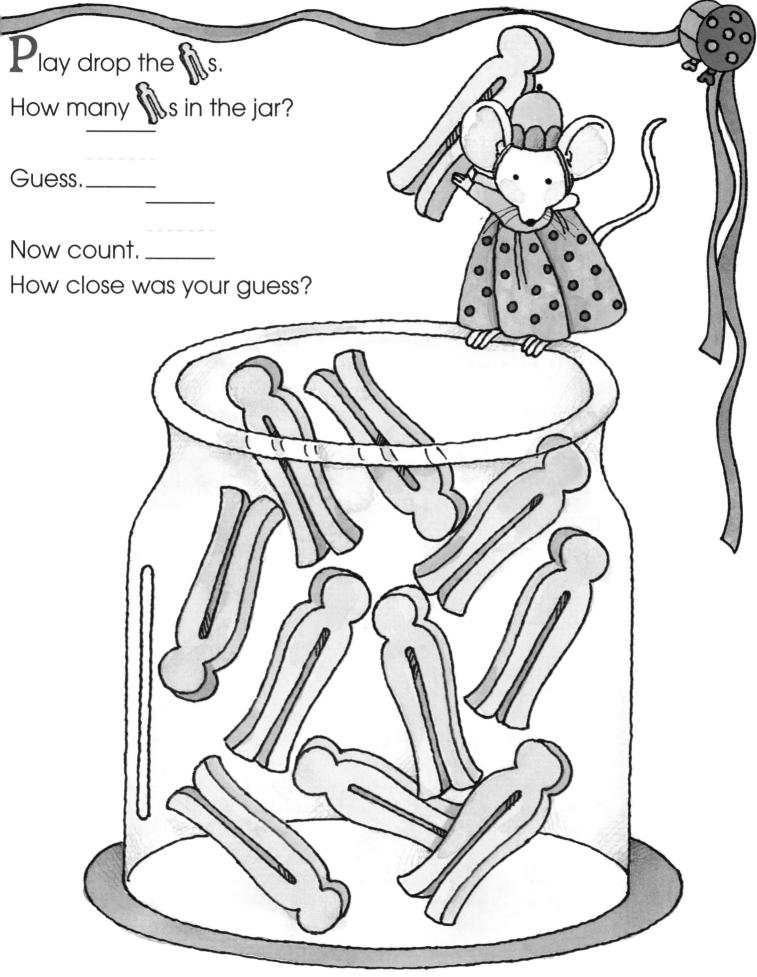s.

How many 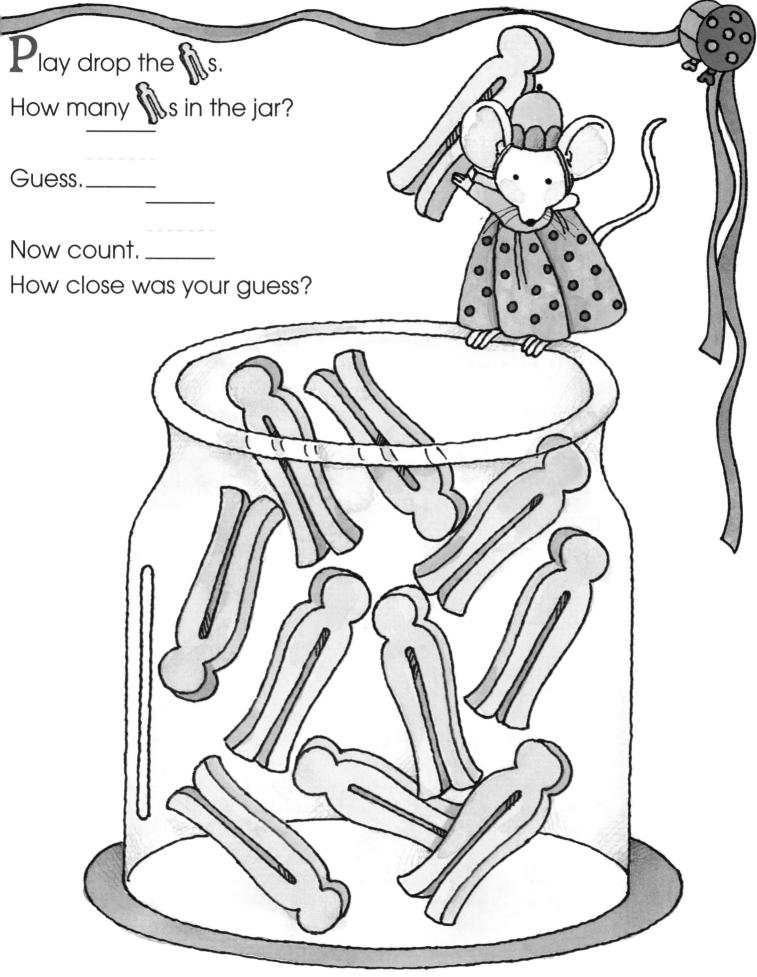s in the jar? _____

Guess. _____
_____

Now count. _____
How close was your guess?

Wow! A juggler!

✏️ lines to the 🎳 that are the same.

Let's play musical chairs.

◯ the 🎉 that is different.

◯ the 🎈 that is different.

◯ the 🪑 that is different.

45

Play the picture sentence game.

◯ the answers.

Look at Dilly's presents!

a line to show what's in each present.

Look at the big photos.

✓ what happened before.

✔ what happened last.

49

Who else came to the party?

 the letters.

T is on the bottom.

A is before T.

C is on top.

◯ the surprise guest.

◯ 2 pictures that rhyme with .
◯ 2 pictures that rhyme with .
◯ 2 pictures that rhyme with .

Here's Dilly's cake.

🖍️ some 🕯️🕯️

🖍️ some 🌹🌹.

✏️ H, B, and D where they belong.

APPY

IRTHDAY

ILLY

Everyone is singing Happy Birthday!

Fill in 1 ☐ for each one you see.

	1	2	3	4	5	6	7	8

Time to eat!

✏️ lines from the kids to what they want.

Nelson wants 1 🍰 and 1 🥛.

Lola wants 2 🍰s and 1 🥛.

Dilly wants 1 🍰, 1 🍫, and 1 🥛.

Ruben

DILLY

Shari

MILK

MILK

Shari wants 1  and 3 🍨s.

Ruben wants 2 🍰s, 1 🍨, and 1 🥛.

What do you want? ✏️ it.

This is a yummy: .

◯ the yummies.

the picture.

How many yummies? _____

Oops! Some things got separated.

lines to what goes together.

DILLY DILLO
12 BAILEY ROAD
PLEASANTVILLE, MI.

HAPPY BIRTHDAY

What's missing from Dilly's toys?

 the rest of each toy.

Then ✏️ the toys.

58

Someone hid the toys!

◯ these toys.

It's time for Nelson, Frank, and Annie to go home.

 their paths.

Dilly

N

F A

Frank

✔ the one with the shortest path.

✘ the two who get home at the same time.

Dilly dreams about his party.

lines to the picture words that rhyme.

There are seven hidden 🕯🕯 in the book. Did you find them?

Trace the number. Then write it.

1

2

3

4

5

Trace the number. Then write it.

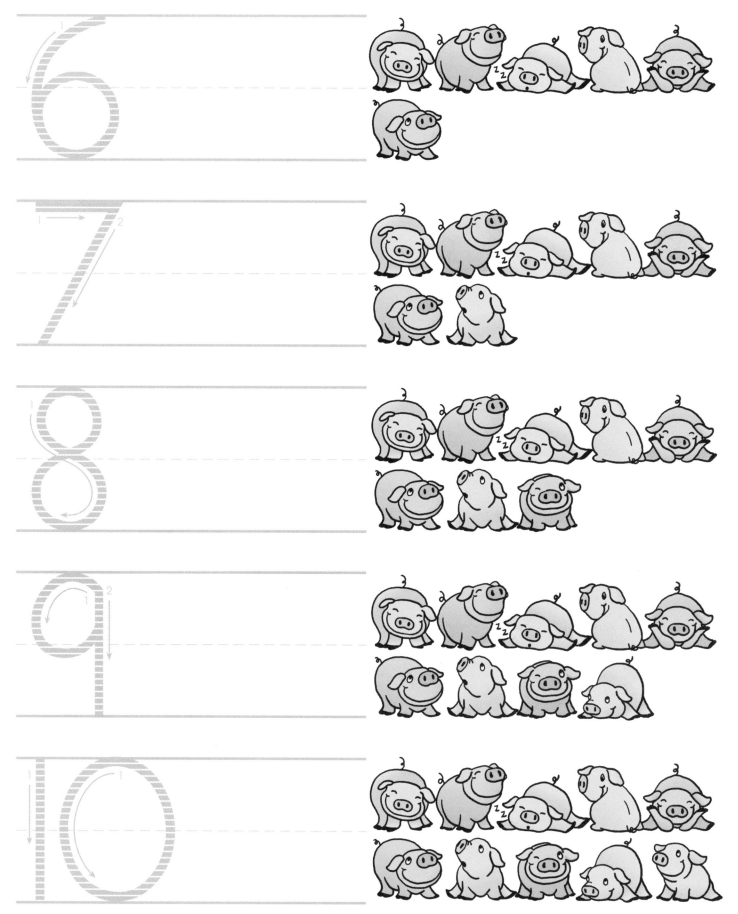

Circle the correct number.

8   9   10

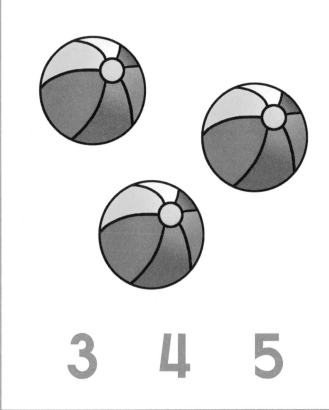

3   4   5

4   5   6

6   7   8

Circle the correct number.

5   6   7

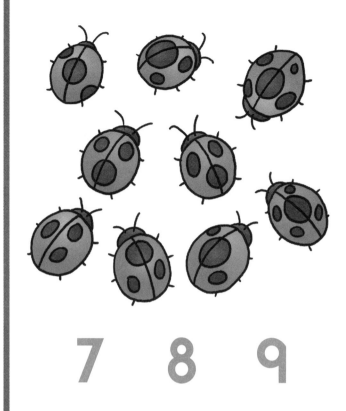

7   8   9

8   9   10

2   3   4

Circle the correct number.

1   2   3

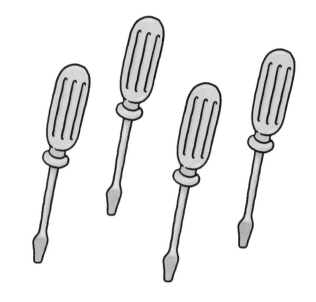

2   3   4

7   8   9

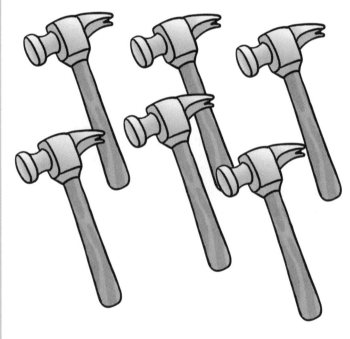

5   6   7

Match the Numbers

Draw a line from each number to the correct group.

1

2

3

4

5

6

7

8

9

10

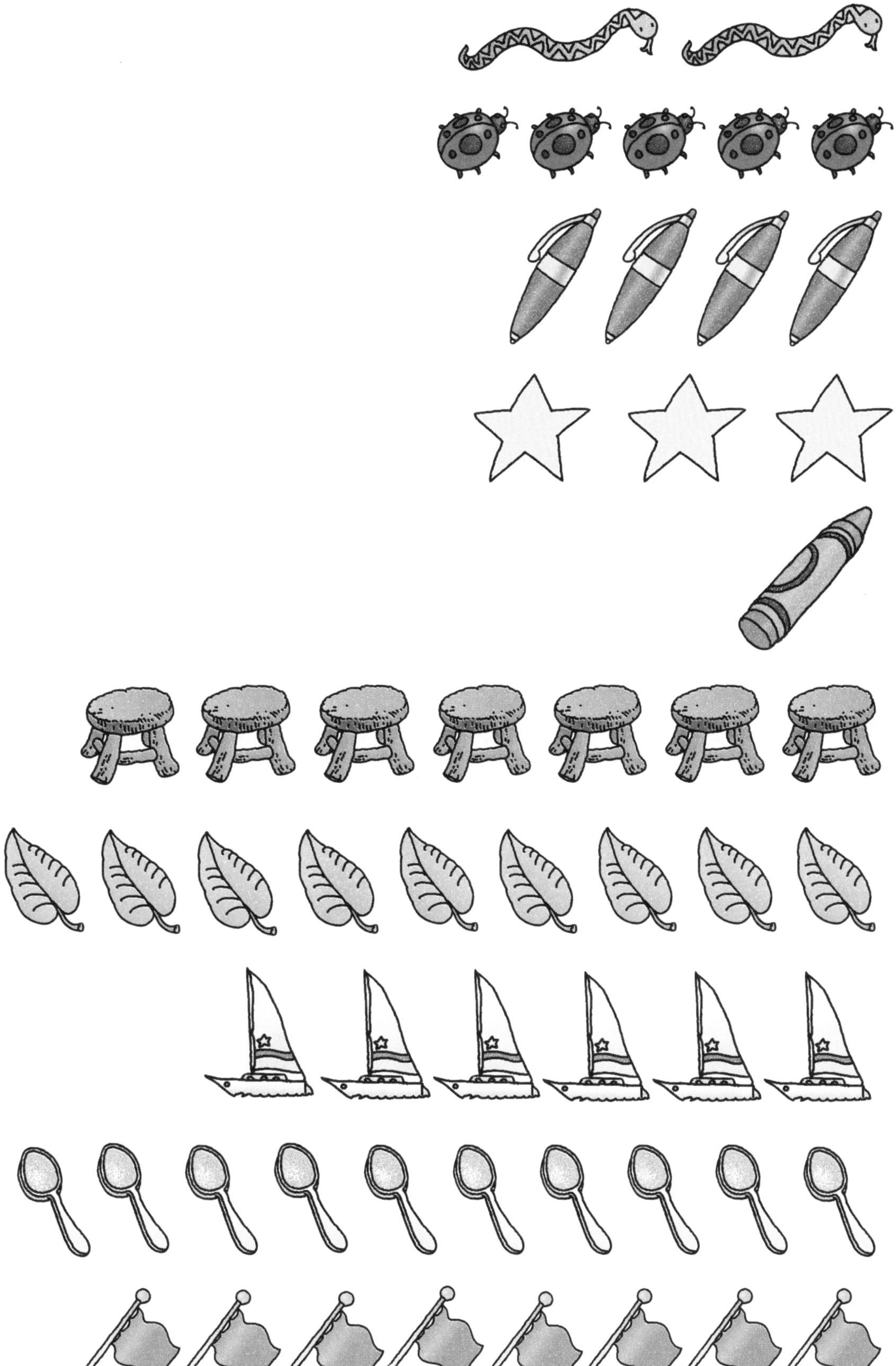

On the Move

1.
one

Circle 1

Circle 1

Circle 1

Out for a Walk

2 ⠂⠂
two

Circle 2 s

Circle 2 s

Circle 2 s

Firefly Frenzy!

3 ...
three

Circle 3 s

Circle 3 s

Circle 3 s

Park Friends

4 ⁞⁞
four

Circle 4 s

Circle 4 s

Circle 4 s

Here, Fishy, Fishy

5 ⠿
five

Circle 5

Circle 5 🐱 s

Circle 5 📚 s

Sounds Pretty!

6 ∴
six

Circle 6 s

Circle 6 s

Circle 6 s

Happy Habitat

7 seven

Circle 7 s

Circle 7 s

Circle 7 s

76

Yummy, Yum!

8
eight

Circle 8 🦋 s

Circle 8 🐞 s

Circle 8 🍎 s

Sea Shells by the Sea Shore

9
nine

Circle 9 s

Circle 9 s

Circle 9 s

Sweet Treat!

10 ∷∷ ten

Circle 10 s

Circle 10 s

Circle 10 s

What is in the Yard?

How many of each are on both pages?
Circle the number.

		2	3	4
s		2	3	4
s		3	4	5
s		1	2	3

How many of each are on both pages?
Circle the number.

		6	7	8
	s	7	8	9
	s	4	5	6
	s	8	9	10

Look at All the Babies!

How many of each kind of baby?

How many of each kind of baby?

s

s

s

s

Count the Animals

Count how many are on both pages. Circle the number.

	4	5	6
s	1	2	3
s	6	7	8

Count how many are on both pages.
Circle the number.

S   2   3   4

S   5   6   7

S   1   2   3

TRY IT!

Make the sounds of different animals. Moo like a cow. Snort like a pig. Cock-a-doodle-do like a rooster!

What Comes Next? _____

What number comes next?

4   5   6   ____

7   8   9   ____

0   1   2   ____

3   4   5   ____

Write the missing numbers.

3 ___ ___ 6 ___ ___

What Comes Next?

What number comes next?
Write the missing numbers.

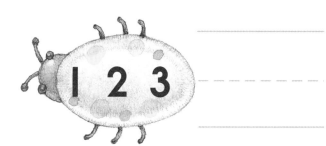 1 2 3

 3 4 5    5 6 7

 7 8 9   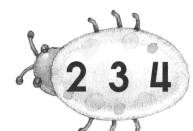 2 3 4

 6 7 8    4 5 6

Write the missing numbers.

1, _____ , 3, 4, 5, _____ , 7, 8, _____

What Comes Before? _____

What number comes before?

Write the missing numbers.

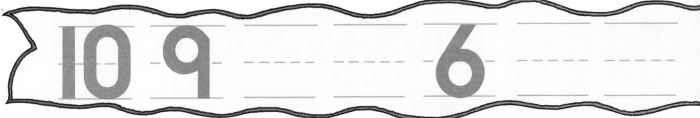

What Comes Before?

What number comes before?
Write the missing numbers.

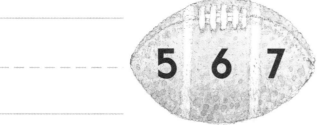

Continue the pattern.

6 , 7 , 8 , 6 , 7 , 8 , 6 , _____ , _____

Fresh from the Bakery

5 is **greater** than 4.

Circle the group that is **greater**.

90

Which Is Greater?

How many are there? Circle the greater number.

(6)　　3

 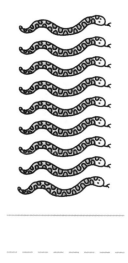  

Circle the number that is greater.

7　3　　6　10　　8　4

School Fun

2 is **less** than 3.

Circle the group that is **less**.

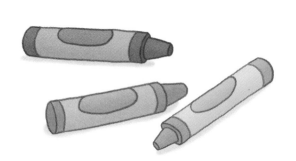 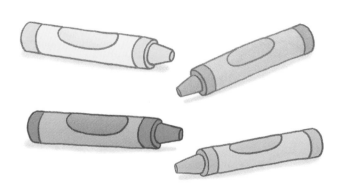

Which Is Less?

How many are there?
Circle the number that is less.

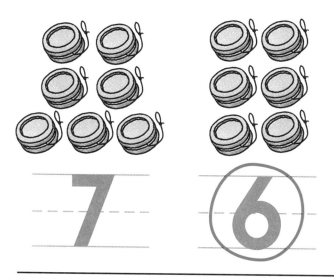

7   (6)

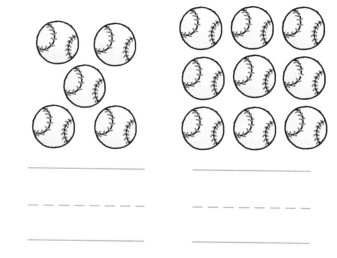

_____   _____

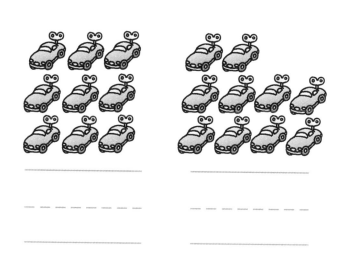

_____   _____

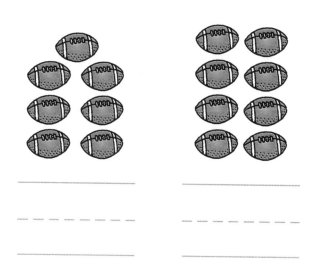

_____   _____

Circle the number that is less.

3 9   4 5   10 6

Your favorite fruit

How many of each thing?

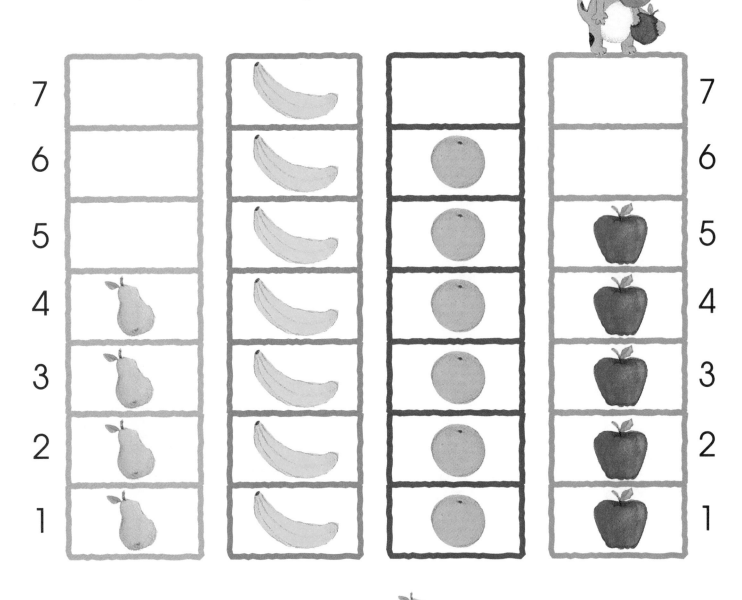

	How many				
How many 🍐s?	3	6	2	4
How many 🍌s?	7	4	3	5
How many 🍊s?	6	3	5	7
How many 🍎s?	4	6	2	5

94

Read the word.
Circle the number that is the same as the word. _____

three   2   4   3   10

five   5   7   4   6

seven   2   10   7   8

one   6   2   10   1

six   8   6   5   9

Read the word.
Circle the number that is the same as the word.

ten   6   10   7   8

four   4   3   6   8

eight   1   2   8   9

two   4   2   3   9

nine   5   1   7   9

Write the correct number on the line.

How many  ? _____

How many ? _____

How many ? _____

Circle the numbers 1-9 hidden in this picture.

Circle five things that are **wrong** with this picture.

Draw a line from each picture to where it **belongs**.

Circle the picture that **does not** belong.

101

Write **1** by what happened **first**.
Write **2** by what happened **next**.
Write **3** by what happened **last**.

Write **1** by what happened **first**.
Write **2** by what happened **next**.
Write **3** by what happened **last**.

Circle **2** that are the **same**.

Circle **2** that are the **same** in each group.

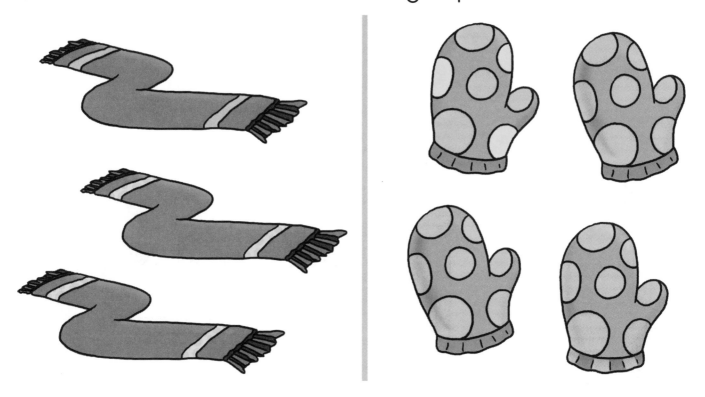

Circle the letters that are the **same** as the first two.

AC	FG	AC
BB	BB	OO
DE	EE	DE
KF	KR	KF

Circle the picture in each row that is **different**.

What **belongs** in each box?
Draw the shapes in the correct color.

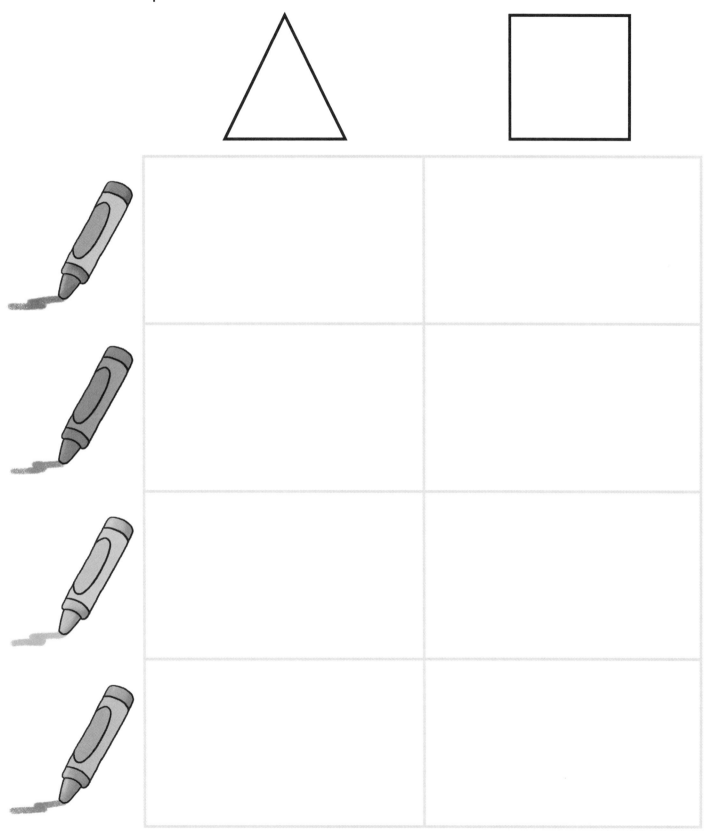

What belongs in each box?
Draw the shapes in the correct color.

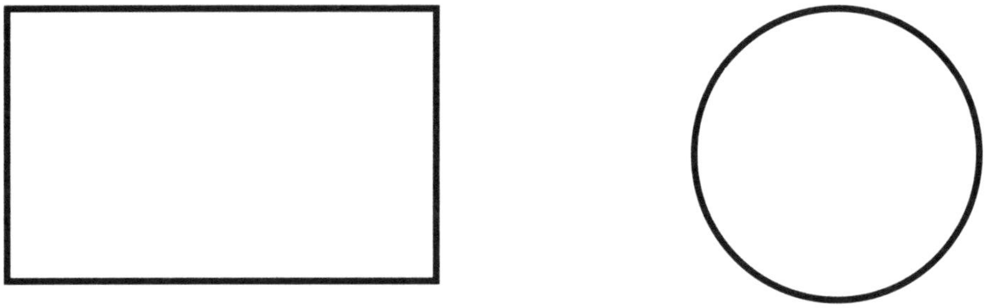

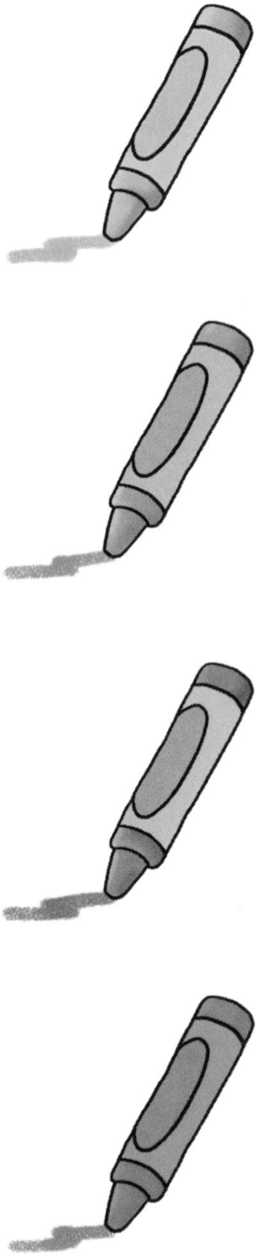

Circle two pictures that go together in each row.

Which frog did John keep?
Circle the correct picture.

1. It has spots.

2. It does not have purple on it.

3. It has yellow on it.

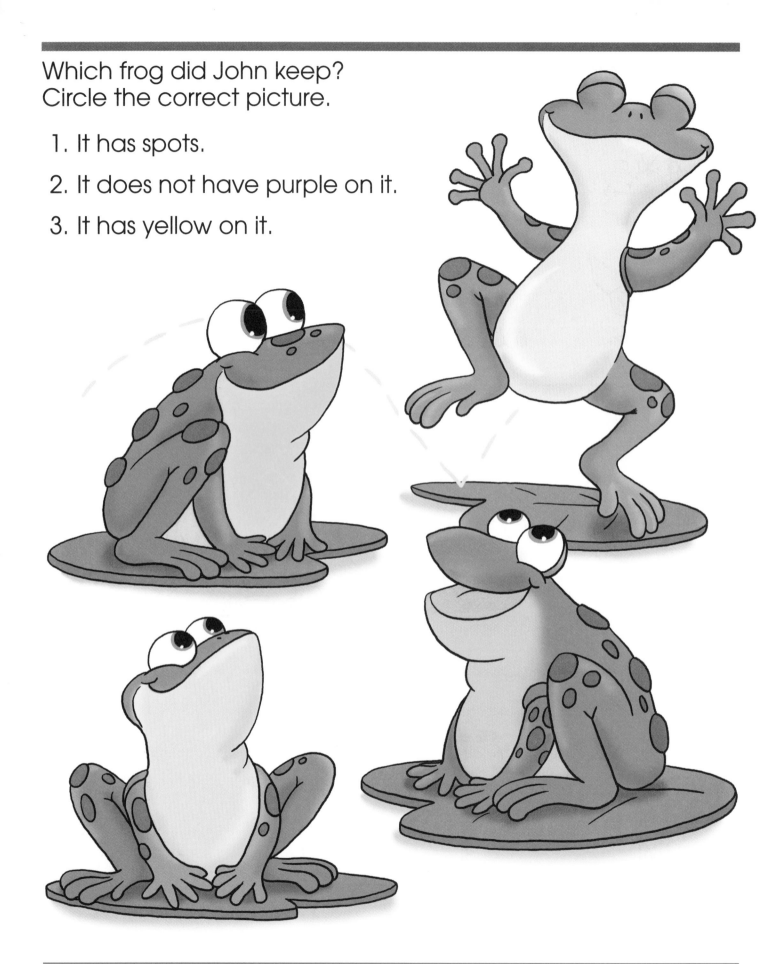

Read the clues.
Draw a line from the name to the correct clown.

1. Mac is between Ned and Jake.

2. Jake has a flower in his hat.

Ned   Jake   Mac

Put an **X** by the picture that shows why this happened.

Circle the picture that shows how you would **feel**.

How many people are going **left**? _____

How many cars are going **right**?_____

Look at clown A.
Circle 7 things that are **different** on clown B?

clown A

clown B

Look at the scene below.
Circle the five hidden images.

117

Circle the picture that shows what will happen **next**.

Look at the pictures in each row.
One thing will be the **same** in all rows.
Circle the sentence that tells what is the
same in each row.

1. The first car has a flat tire.

2. The last car has a bent bumper.

3. The middle car is the same color.

Look at the pictures in each row.
One thing will be the **same** in all rows.
Circle the sentence that tells what is the
same in each row.

1. All apples are red.

2. All rows have a pineapple.

3. The last fruit in each row is a banana.

Double Vision

Circle the pictures that are the **same** size.

Beautiful Blue

 the  blue.

Color what is **blue**.

Yipee for Yellow

 the ☼ yellow.

Color what is yellow.

123

Real Red

 the 🍎 red.

Color what is **red**.

Perfect Purple

Color the 🖍️ the 🍆 **purple**.

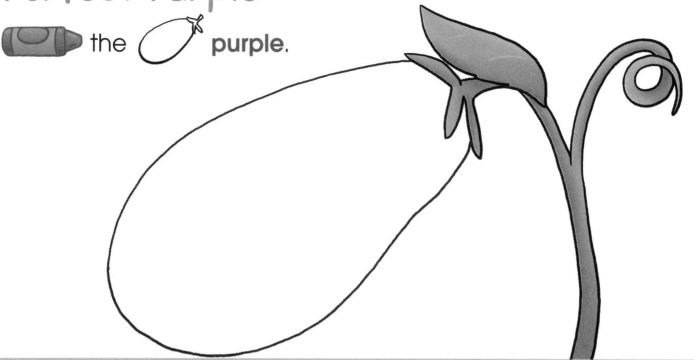

Color what is **purple**.

Outstanding Orange

🖍 the 🥕 orange.

Color what is orange.

Green Is Great

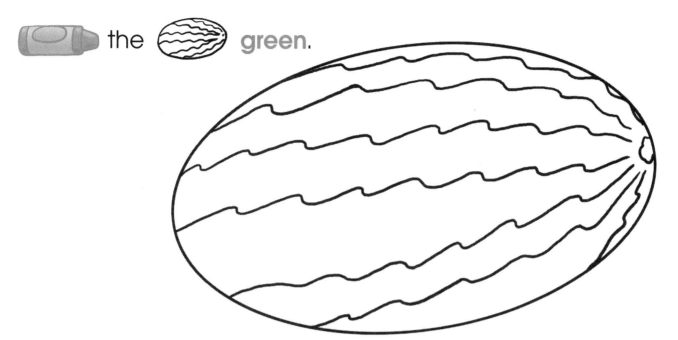

the 🍉 green.

Color what is **green**.

Learning Award

Great Job!

_____
Name

Finished
Preschool
DVD Book
from
School Zone Publishing.